Why Are You Always on the Phone?

Why Are You Always on the Phone?

SMART Skills with the Smartphone Generation

Dr. Michelle M L Yeo
UniSIM, Singapore

World Scientific

NEW JERSEY · LONDON · SINGAPORE · BEIJING · SHANGHAI · HONG KONG · TAIPEI · CHENNAI ·

World Scientific Publishing Co. Pte. Ltd.
5 Toh Tuck Link, Singapore 596224
USA office: 27 Warren Street, Suite 401-402, Hackensack, NJ 07601
UK office: 57 Shelton Street, Covent Garden, London WC2H 9HE

British Library Cataloguing-in-Publication Data
A catalogue record for this book is available from the British Library.

WHY ARE YOU ALWAYS ON THE PHONE?
SMART Skills with the Smartphone Generation

Copyright © 2017 by World Scientific Publishing Co. Pte. Ltd.

All rights reserved. This book, or parts thereof, may not be reproduced in any form or by any means, electronic or mechanical, including photocopying, recording or any information storage and retrieval system now known or to be invented, without written permission from the publisher.

For photocopying of material in this volume, please pay a copying fee through the Copyright Clearance Center, Inc., 222 Rosewood Drive, Danvers, MA 01923, USA. In this case permission to photocopy is not required from the publisher.

ISBN 978-981-3149-33-5
ISBN 978-981-3149-34-2 (pbk)

Desk Editor: Jiang Yulin

Typeset by Stallion Press
Email: enquiries@stallionpress.com

DEDICATION

To Branson Tay with love, thanks for adding me on Facebook, keeping me updated with your social life and friends and for the lovely mother-and-son quality time together. This book is inspired by these special moments. Look forward to more endearing moments together in the future.

Special mention to my husband, Terrance Tay, my pillar of strength, for standing by me during the difficult moments at home and encouraging me to stay on track to complete writing this book.

A warm thank-you to the parents for sharing their experiences, opinions and even good parenting tips. Thanks to wonderful colleagues/educators who have shared their professional tips and experiences amidst their busy schedules.

A special thank-you to all the tweens/teens and the wonderful bunch of Bukit Panjang primary students, Tanglin secondary students, Outram secondary students and Nanyang polytechnic students for their kind contributions without which the content of this book would not be complete.

Thanks to Dr Charles Ong, Mr Andrew Lim and Mr Samuthiran for so kindly spending valuable time reading, reviewing and providing helpful and insightful feedback to improve the content of this book. Cheers to the years of friendship and the camaraderie with you all!

Last but not least, to all my readers, enjoy the read and I hope you will find the suggestions and tips useful and helpful when bonding with your tweens/teens.

CONTENTS

Dedication   v
Synopsis   ix
Introduction — SMART Skills   xi

S for SOCIAL   1
ONE — Why Are You Always on the Phone?   3
TWO — My Teen Seems Addicted to the Phone   7

M for MANAGEMENT   11
THREE — How Should I Limit My Tween/Teen's Game Playing Hours?   13
FOUR — Phone Privacy: Should I Be Reading His or Her Text Messages?   17
FIVE — Social Media, Social Life: How Teens View Their Digital Lives?   19
SIX — Tweens/Teens Like Face-to-Face Communication and Texting   23

A for AWARENESS   25
SEVEN — Awkward Online-Parenting Moments: How Do I Talk About Internet Porn?   27
EIGHT — Serious Smartphone and Online Problems: Digital Harassment   31
NINE — How to Respond to Haters and Trolls Online?   33
TEN — Cyber-Bullying: What If My Tween/Teen Is Cyber-Bullied?   37
ELEVEN — How Should I Go about Discussing Safe Online Behavior?   43

R for RECIPROCAL   47
TWELVE — How Do I Monitor without "Spying"?: A Balanced Approach   49

THIRTEEN — Should I Friend or Unfriend My Tweens/Teens
on Social Media? 53
FOURTEEN — What Apps Are Good for Learning?: Pros and Cons? 55
FIFTEEN — Is It OK to Start His/Her Own YouTube Channel? 59
SIXTEEN — Mean YouTube Comments Are Upsetting 61
SEVENTEEN — Constant Multi-Tasking during Homework? 63
EIGHTEEN — How to Be a Responsible "Instagrammer"? 65
NINETEEN — What Should We Know about Twittering? 67
TWENTY — Tumblr and Concerns with Using Tumblr 69
TWENTY-ONE — Snapchat?: Here Today; Gone Tomorrow? 73

T for TACT 75
TWENTY-TWO — Communicating for a Better Relationship 77
TWENTY-THREE — Epilogue 83

Endnotes 85

SYNOPSIS

Why Are You Always on the Phone? SMART Skills with the Smartphone Generation is a revelation and an actual depiction of what goes on in the everyday lives of youth who are connected and are online most of the time either via their smartphone or their iPad. Many a time, parents of tweens and teenagers from the age of 10 onwards to 18, are curious and are even "tearing their hair out"; frustrated with their child/children's obsession with texting and chatting online 24/7. The challenge then is how we can seek to understand the complexities and nuances of our youth and their connection in the 21st-century technologically driven globalized society. Unraveling this challenge, this book provides powerful insights into the lives of individuals as they grapple with the rise of being connected at any time and at any place via their smartphone. Voices from parents, tweens and teens sharing their online experiences and opinions have been weaved and compiled into the text for an honest and interesting read for all.

With stories and anecdotes, *Why Are You Always on the Phone?* serves to answer the questions "Why are you always online?", "What are you doing online?" and a list of queries that most parents, educators and even tweens and teenagers themselves seek to know and are curious about. It is hoped that by answering these, it will prompt deeper, more empathetic, and layered connections between parents, tweens, teenagers and educators for more fulfilling parent-child and teacher-student relationships and thus highlight the importance of practising effective and safe uses of the smartphone and other devices.

INTRODUCTION — SMART SKILLS

This book is written and organized according to the abbreviation "**SMART**" for the skills needed to deal with the smartphone generation. **S** stands for **Social**, **M** stands for **Management**, **A** stands for **Awareness**, **R** for **Reciprocal** and **T** for **Tact**. The book begins with **S** for **Social** — human beings are social creatures and so are the tweens and teens of today. This section defines youth and who they are. And it continues with an understanding of how parents can be friends with their tweens/teens online and offline with some snippets of some concerns and parents' voices. **M** is for **Management** — that of managing online presence and identity and having good time management with online and offline activities. This section discusses how parents can manage their use of the smartphone to be a good role model of online presence, too. **A** for **Awareness** which is being aware of the pros and cons of these online connections; being aware of the dangers and issues of using the social media applications and the know-hows to deal with cyber-bullying and trolls, etc. The letter **R** is for **Reciprocal** and on building relationship which is reciprocal be it between peers for the teens and between parents and their child/children. There is a need for quality time with quality activities with tweens/teens' interests at heart in order to build a good relationship. **T** is for **Tact** which is about how to be tactful towards peers and on setting rules on the uses of the smartphone and being tactful with postings as well as dealing tactfully with issues and mean comments online. There is the coverage of tips for parents to spend quality time and use affirmative words with teens to build a loving and wonderful parent-child relationship.

S for
Social

ONE

WHY ARE YOU ALWAYS ON THE PHONE?

Staying in touch with friends is of utmost importance to teenagers — when we were teens, we talked for hours on the phone, too! Now the same kind of contact happens through phone texting. And, as annoying as it can be to see our son/daughter tapping away at their phones, it is a normal part of life for tweens (8 to 12 years old) and teens (13 to 19 years old).

According to Lynn Schofield Clark,[1] children and youth of today belong to the "constant connect" generation and they are using any opportunity of private spaces and time online to experience with identities, seek advice on personal matters from their friends and peers, or to listen in and read the interactions of the group chat via their smartphone. Indeed, although most adults would find it quizzical why these tweens and teens are constantly on their phones, it is nevertheless a highly valued social activity for them to be chatting, to be engaged in uninterrupted, unobserved moments, and to be immersed in peer communication. As Sherry Turkle[2] in her book *Reclaiming Conversation* suggests, it is more useful to consider the ways in which technology can make us vulnerable to undesirable behaviors such as multi-tasking or hurting our conversations with others. In fact, teens check their devices frequently and are sometimes pressed to respond quickly to their friend's messages. But while it looks like they are addicted and some may really even feel so, this is apparently observed as normal for any tween or teenager as they are going through a phase in life when friends take priority over everything else.

However, if smartphone use is getting in the way of family time, homework, grades and other responsibilities, it might be time to help your tween/teen manage his or her phone time. The following are tips to smart-management skills with smartphones:

1. **Help your tween/teen find time for face-to-face conversations.** Designate a fixed time, say for 30 to 45 minutes that is no phone contact time but pure communication with face-to-face conversation.

2. **If your tween/teen prefers to text than talk,** create a family group mobile chat using "WhatsApp" and have them know that you would like to be in touch with one another as a family. Then you can understand the text "language" and keep in touch with your tween/teen, and to even send reminder to put away the phone for a short duration, if possible.

3. **Ask your tween/teen to put down the mobile/cell phone during main conversation times at dinner** or during car rides to and from school or being at the football field/ swimming pool or the music school.

4. **Ask and talk to him/her firmly but politely on the house rules and the safety rules of using of mobile/cell phones as you would with a friend or co-worker.**

5. **Most importantly, you have to be the role model** for the manners and behaviors that you want to see from your tween/teen with their phone uses.

In fact, parents themselves are displaying their frequent smartphone use to their tweens/teens. While most of us would like to think we have a healthy relationship with our tweens/teens (and our phones), the facts do not back us up. But what is really going on? Sure, many of us are sneaking a Facebook update at the music school's or karate studio's carpark. This is to help kill some time while waiting, or scrolling through email while sitting through the school homework bonding time with your kid. Still, if we as parents are going to be smart about our smartphone usage, we do need to make a few rules for ourselves — just as we make the house rules for our tween/teen on smartphone uses. Smartphone users tend to underestimate the time they spend staring at their phones instead of interacting with their tweens/teens. It might feel like 20 seconds, but in reality, three minutes have passed — long enough for your tween/teen to wander off, get into trouble, or feel neglected.

Here are a few recommendations to keeping our relationship with our smartphone more balanced:

1. **No devices or smartphone during mealtimes. And if a topic comes up that you would normally google, add it to a list to look up later.**

2. **Leave the game-playing** (even Candy Crush) until after your tweens/teens are in bed.

3. **No texting or talking on the phone in the car or when spending quality time with your tween/teen.**
4. **Designate "no-tech zones" in your home** — and respect this rule.
5. **Designate a fixed place** (a bowl, holder or tray where all phones and electronic devices such as iPad are placed when they are being charged or kept).

And remember, you are modeling behavior for your children. So if you do not want your tween or teen to be glued or addicted to the phone, try not to act like one yourself. But, do make sure to excuse yourself if you need to interrupt the family conversation moment to attend to your phone (only for an in-coming call, or for Global Positioning System (GPS) guidance to look up directions to an event).

What some parents say:

> I agree with the comment about modeling behavior you want to see. I have witnessed many adults who are as glued to their phone in a public situation as children — I personally find this rude. I also think today's children are really up against it, phones are very entertaining and addictive, but, can we really give them these devices and expect them not to be incredibly drawn to them, or are we just setting them up?

Mrs Jayathanthi, *early 40s,*
Assistant Manager

> You would like your child to put down his or her phone? Put yours down. Children watch and learn, they do not listen and learn. Ever heard? Actions speak louder than words? THEY DO.

Mrs Tan SH, *mid 30s, Homemaker*

TWO
MY TEEN SEEMS ADDICTED TO THE PHONE

Addiction is a complex subject, and though it may be tempting to point to young peoples' evolving technology- and media-related behaviors as evidence of new addictions, it is vital to sift out true addictions which reflect severe problems with very specific medical criteria. We should not be too easy and quick to point at our tween/teen's smartphone and media use as an addiction. As parents, it would be good to be aware of the problems and issues of social media use which could affect our tween/teen, either negatively or positively, socially and emotionally. Obsession with online gaming was the main manifestation in the past, but addiction to social media and video downloading, also known as digital addiction, are now on the uptrend.

Digital addiction is slowly becoming serious and according to psychiatrists in Singapore, they are pushing for medical authorities to formally recognize addiction to the Internet and digital devices as a disorder, joining other countries around the world in addressing a growing problem.

In terms of physical symptoms, the common ailment is referred to as "Text-Neck" or "i-Neck" pain — according to Tan Kian Hian, a consultant at the Anesthesiology Department of Singapore General Hospital — as it is an observed phenomenon from the lowering of smartphone users' heads and using of their mobile devices constantly on the go, while queuing and even crossing the roads.

Trisha Lin, an Assistant Professor in Communications at the Nanyang Technological University, Singapore, defined digital addiction by these symptoms:

1. The inability to control craving;
2. Anxiety when separated from a smartphone;
3. Loss in productivity in studies or at work;
4. The need to constantly check one's phone.

So what can be done to overcome this addiction? In the medical profession, some doctors do not really agree whether people can become addicted to their smartphone or technology, unless of course, the issues of malnutrition and not eating or working because of the exhaustive and long hours on their electronic devices surface. Hopefully, you are only dealing with your tween/teen's compulsive habit that you can manage but if you suspect the problem is true addiction, and is causing a lot of physical and mental distress, talk to a medical doctor, a psychologist or a school counseling team. In Singapore, there are two counseling centers with programs for digital addiction. They are the National Addictions Management Services[3] and Touch Community Services[4] with programs to prevent digital addiction.

Additionally, you can try out the following tips to help tweens/teens and even yourself to overcome digital addiction on your own:

1. Stop for a moment whenever the phone vibrates or rings and ask the following questions: Why am I checking the phone? For text messages? For update of social media? Or for replying to an email?
2. Prioritize. Reply only to urgent messages quickly or call back as a reply and leave the more casual and social messages till after work is done or at rest times. Or reply to messages just **three** times a day.
3. For update of social media notification, do it only via the computer at certain times of the day.
4. Mute phone notification, including the group's "WhatsApp" messages. This prevents distractions. Reading and responding to these notifications do take up lots of time. Hence, read and reply only at specific times of the day; that are set aside for such updates.
5. Set specific boundaries for smartphone usage. Limit the usage by setting specific no phone usage during these times:

    — At mealtimes;
    — At social events;
    — At work;
    — In the washroom/restroom;
    — During face-to-face conversations.

6. Use apps to track and restrict smartphone usage. The three recommended apps are:

— RescueTime (Android)[5]: This app helps you understand your phone usage patterns. It gives a detailed breakdown of how much time you spend using different categories of apps.

— Moment (iOS)[6]: This app enables you to track how much you have used on your iPhone and iPad. It can help you set daily usage limits and notifications when these limits are reached.

— AppDetox (Android)[7]: AppDetox allows you to set phone usage rules. It can limit the checking of email at a certain time and it can limit the frequency of opening the text message app among other types of restrictions.

7. **Establish consequences for problematic phone use.** For example, if your tweens/teens are not able to put the phone away when you ask or are engaged in other problematic phone-related behavior, then consider a temporary time or location limit. Employ a last resort measure of a complete ban until attitudes change for the better. You can also contact your mobile phone subscribers to let you set daily phone-use limits, and download some apps that can disable your tween/teen's phone when he or she hits a limit.

THREE

HOW SHOULD I LIMIT MY TWEEN/TEEN'S GAME PLAYING HOURS?

Popular games — Stack, Crossy Road, Clash Royale, Clash of Clans, Color Switch, Piano Tiles, Candy Crush, Subway Surfers, Plants vs. Zombies and 2048 — are but some of the games that tweens and teens like to play on their smartphone. But is it OK to play these games for hours? The same goes for computer games such as first-person shooters (FPS) like Black Shot, Counter-Strike, and indie-genre games like Minecraft.

Minecraft? To put simply, it is an open-ended building game with seemingly endless possibilities, although this game can be very time-consuming. In fact, most of these games provide the thrill, the "feel good" positive and rewarding gratification with each successful attempt. As parents, it would be interesting to find out what these games are and to know how difficult it is to stop playing once you like it.

Try looking up and playing these games. It helps you to better understand the gamer in your tween/teen. On the plus side, Minecraft for example, can reinforce

geometry concepts as it strengthens players' thinking and reasoning skills, creativity, and even collaboration. The game has a strong, positive online community and even has an educational module that teachers can modify for classroom lessons on different subjects. On the downside, as you have discovered, it does take up a huge chunk of time.

The other very highly acclaimed mobile augmented-reality game and one of the hottest apps in the world currently, Pokémon Go, created by Niantic, is a huge hit with players since its first launch. This game had even rocketed to become the No. 1 free app in Apple's US iTune store when it first launched in the first week of July 2016. What makes this game so popular and addictive is that it involves users physically going to landmarks where they can see and interact with objects like Poké Balls and Pokémon. Pokémon Go effectively turns the real world into the setting for the game.

The geographical mapping feature in Pokémon Go is leading players to areas/locations that may be secluded or prohibited places. This may pose as a problem and danger of players getting physically hurt and as an easy target of some law-offenders at secluded spots. The app also uses a player's location data with no opt out for this feature and hence, this raises privacy issues as the player's location will be made known. There is no way to shut the location's information off. Another risk players should be aware is that as they log into the app using Google, they are actually also giving permission for the app to have access to information on their Google account!

Although Pokémon Go app itself is free, players may end up with making actual cash payments and spending a lot of money unwittingly. Players need to build their Pokémon inventory, which leads to spending money to store, train, hatch and battle. With PokéCoins, the in-game currency of Pokémon Go, players need these coins to buy useful items, such as Poké Balls, which are needed to actually "catch" Pokémon, as well as for inventory upgrades. There are ways to earn coins within the flow of the game, but the fastest way is to purchase using real cash. Players can easily pay anywhere from US 99 cents for 100 PokéCoins to US$99.99 for 14,500 coins.

How can we get round to playing Pokémon Go safely?

- To prevent your tween/teen from spending a fortune on the Pokémon universe, you can add parental controls against in-app spending with Ask to Buy.[8]
- Players should also make sure they are downloading the correct version of the game, on Apple Store or Google Play; there have been some reports of games made to look like Pokémon Go that are infecting mobile devices. Hence, try not to download any app from a third-party app market that is not owned by Apple or Google.
- Last but not least, you should consider playing the game together with your tween/teen. This is one of the ways to bond with him or her and to have an increased awareness of this game.

Even "good" games can be played to excess, and homework, chores, family obligations, and real-world social activities can take a backseat when your tween/teen cannot or would not stop playing. And even if he or she is learning from the game, other areas of life are equally important, too. What should you do? Here are some tips:

1. **Start by having a conversation about the games and how you have tried playing these games.** Then, advise them on knowing when to stop playing and to continue with other duties, and figuring out how much game time fits in.
2. **Help your tween/teen self-regulate;** help him or her set up a play and study time-table.
3. **Create a calendar together and have them set a timer.** Praise and reward them for following through to the time limits. It is a matter of trust that your tween/teen

is following through with the time-tabling. However, if he or she does not or cannot follow by the time, then the time will have to be taken away from the next day or week.

An example of a weekly time-table is shown below.

Days	Events	Remarks
Monday	1. Finish the wiki project in school 2. Jamming session with the Jetsons	Bring research materials to school for discussion.
Tuesday	1. Study Astrology 2. Finish Chemistry paper	
Wednesday	Do ….	
Thursday	Learn how to ….	
Friday	Wash my clothes	
Saturday	Study Physics	
Sunday	Family time and no phone day from 2 to 3 pm	

The following is an example of a weekly time-table template.

Days	Events	Remarks
Monday		
Tuesday		
Wednesday		
Thursday		
Friday		
Saturday		
Sunday		

FOUR

PHONE PRIVACY: SHOULD I BE READING HIS OR HER TEXT MESSAGES?

There is no absolutely right answer here. It depends on your tween/teen's age, personality, and behavior. The most important thing is that you discuss responsible texting behavior. Remind them that any text can be forwarded to an unintended audience — and texts that involve drugs, sexting, or other illegal things can get them into real trouble.

The ideal time to establish rules around how the phone will be monitored is at the very beginning, when you give it to him or her. It is then easier to relax your rules as you go along, rather than suddenly introduce new ones.

Here are some ways to smart text-messaging parenting skills:

1. **You can simply ask to see their messages.** If your kids recoil in horror, you may try asking why they do not want you to see them — most times, it is very likely that there is nothing bad.
2. **You can start by asking or checking with his or her friends.** Do so if you have reason to suspect that there is something dodgy that he or she would not discuss and you notice changes in his or her behavior, appearance, and actions.
3. **You can consider purchasing a text-monitoring service** through your phone service-provider/carrier. Alternatively, you can also use apps such as RescueTime (Android), Moment (iOS) or AppDetox (Android) to restrict smartphone usage.
4. **Discuss appropriate smartphone user behavior and set consequences** for not abiding by these house rules. Thereafter, continue to monitor your tween/teen's behavior by the side. Every parent faces this dilemma at one time or another, whether it is regarding text messages or Facebook posts. If you do decide to sneak a peek, be prepared to see things you may not really like and to choose whether or not to confront your child about what you have discovered.

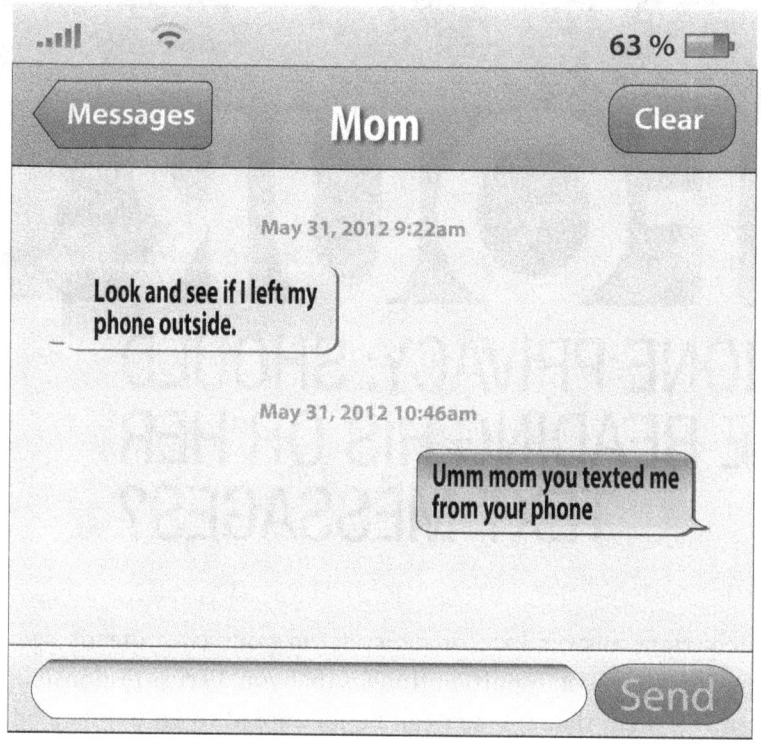

FIVE

SOCIAL MEDIA, SOCIAL LIFE: HOW TEENS VIEW THEIR DIGITAL LIVES?

According to interviews with teens in Singapore on how they view their digital lives, many more teens report a positive impact of social media use on their emotional well-being than a negative one. Most teens do not think their use of social media affects their social and emotional well-being one way or the other. But there are some teens who think that using social media does affect how they feel about themselves and their social situation.

At least one in four teens say that using their social networking site makes them feel less shy and more outgoing; one in five say it makes them feel more confident, more popular, and more sympathetic to others; and 15% say it makes them feel better about themselves. By comparison, only a few teens say social networking makes them feel less outgoing; 4% feel worse about themselves, less confident, and less popular after using their social networking site; and 3% feel shyer.

Very few teens think that using their social network site makes them more depressed. Among all teen social network users, only 5% say using their social networking site makes them feel more depressed, compared to 10% who say it makes them feel less depressed. Even among the least happy teens in this study (the 10% of all teens who say they are often sad or depressed and are not very happy with their lives), 18% say using their social networking site makes them feel more depressed, while 13% say it lessens their depression.

In particular, teens think that using social media has helped their relationships. Half of all teen social media users say using such media has mainly helped their relationships with friends, compared to just 4% who say social media use has mainly hurt their relationships. Similarly, more than a third of the teens say social media use has mainly helped their relationships with family members, compared to 2% who say it has mainly hurt them. In addition, a majority of teens say social media has helped them to keep in touch with friends they cannot see regularly, get to know other students at their school better, and connect with new people who share a common interest.

Interestingly, quite some number of teens who are social media users say they have flirted with someone online that they would not have flirted with in person, and a minority say they would have said something bad about someone online that they would not have said in person.

Teens are using social media applications mainly for social purposes of networking, relaxation, entertainment reasons such as watching and making videos for fun, and just purely connecting with what is happening currently. The following are other reasons raised by teens on why they use social media:

- Lots and lots of information and resources;

- Social media is engaging and it is definitely interesting to be connected 24/7 during and after school at any time;

- Many things that one can do at "own time, own target" pace;

- Friends would usually "request" to be added on Facebook and to follow one another via Instagram.

In short, teens are online all the time and always on the phone through these connections. Teens like to be connected with one another using Facebook to make friends and to learn from one another. They also like to use YouTube videos for informal learning — the learning of information and knowledge that extends beyond the knowledge learnt in school and from the textbook. They feel that with the rich connectivity with many people and friends online, "that learning … would be an enriching experience that no textbooks could provide".

What the teens say:

> I like the sharing and communication ... for knowledge of the world than just information from the textbooks and curriculum ... In fact, learning can take place at anytime and anyplace on Facebook.

Evan, *18 years old*

> I like the social interactive aspect of sharing and openly discussing interesting topics on Facebook and preparing myself for the real working world ... Learning using Facebook postings would be an enriching experience that no textbooks could provide ... I learn much more from Facebook as more people are interlinked and connected.

John, *16 years old*

> I would sometimes learn life's experiences through watching the YouTube videos, things such as life skills, knowledge of how to prepare for job interview, or even knowing basic social etiquette skills ... I can access websites that teach me skills like, video-editing or how to make my profile look good for my career in future.

Dorothy, *17 years old*

Darren, *19 years old*

It will be a good learning tool if the YouTube videos are well recommended by classmates, friends and teachers ... the videos can be used as good and engaging teaching aids ... When tutors suggest and recommend the websites and links on Facebook for learning, then it is a good learning tool for students.

SIX

TWEENS/TEENS LIKE FACE-TO-FACE COMMUNICATION AND TEXTING

Despite being avid social media users, talking to each other in person is still tweens/teens' favorite way to communicate in Singapore. Nearly 80% of all the tweens/teens interviewed say their favorite way to communicate with their friends is in person, in class or at the canteen. Texting is the next favorite (60%), with social networking (30%), talking on the phone (10%), and Twitter (2%) far behind.

In the following, tweens/teens voice their preference for face-to-face conversations[9]:

- Chatting face-to-face is more fun with real laughter and expressions and we can understand what people really mean in person;
- Can gossip without getting caught in writing;
- In case messages get sent to the wrong person, so it is safer to talk directly on the phone or in person.

On the other hand, some teens highlight their reasons for preferring to texting:

- Texting is faster and easier ... easier than talking ...;
- There is more time to think about how to respond to some messages;
- Texting is more personal and less awkward;
- Can be more open and chat more seriously sometimes.

How about problems and issues with using these social media applications? The following illustrate what most of the teens think:

- Somehow using social media takes away time from doing other stuff ... like spending quality time with people face-to-face;
- Using these social media often distracts me from the people I'm with in person;
- Many tweens/teens recognize that they and their friends as well as family members are increasingly "stuck" to their electronic gadgets, and a small number of the tweens/teens express a desire to disconnect sometimes. As one teen comments, "Sometimes it is nice to just chill and relax, and not talking or sharing anything with anyone ... a minute kind of silence thingy without FB ... ";
- Among tweens/teens who own a smartphone, a majority of them answer "yes" when asked whether they would describe themselves as "addicted" to their phones (though addiction is identified here, this certainly does not imply a clinical addiction condition);
- Some teens even feel frustrated by how attached their friends and parents are to their own devices. For example, some teens say that they may consider their parents "addicted" to their gadgets, and a few others echo similar sentiments that they wish their parents would spend less time with their smartphone and other devices, too.

Social media use does affect how some teens interact with one another and there is indeed a myriad of issues and problems. However, having a sense of awareness of these can help ease one's concern. You can find, in the subsequent chapters, tips and advice on how best to tackle some of these online issues, problems and concerns.

A for
Awareness

SEVEN
AWKWARD ONLINE-PARENTING MOMENTS: HOW DO I TALK ABOUT INTERNET PORN?

There is no sugarcoating it. Internet pornography is easy access for all even through completely innocent searches. Half of teens in Singapore are exposed to pornography, according to a survey published in the Straits Times.[10] According to the survey conducted by Touch Cyber Wellness in 2016 — with a sample size of 921 students aged 13 to 15 years old with 479 boys and 442 girls — nine in every 10 teenage boys in Singapore have watched or read sexually explicit materials within the past year with some first exposed to it even before they start primary school. In contrast, only 8% of girls — less than one in 10 — admitted to viewing pornography last year, either intentionally or by accident.

When asked how they were first exposed to pornography, 54% of the boys said they searched for it intentionally via the Internet while 43% of the girls stumbled upon it while surfing online. And according to the survey, the main mode of accessing pornographic materials is through personal mobile devices. Experts say the findings are worrying as such content can affect children's studies, self-esteem, interpersonal relationships and their attitudes and behavior towards love and sex. If addiction sets in, it may lead to various forms of dysfunctions and sexual crimes. Touch Cyber Wellness manager Chong Ee Jay called the figures "expectedly alarming".

Many parents may find themselves confronting this issue much sooner than they imagined, with tweens/teens who may not even understand exactly what sex is. To begin with, advice or discussion is best done in privacy or somewhere away from a crowded place. It may probably be best talking about it in the car, where nobody has to make eye contact. Depending on how comfortable or miserable your tween/teen may feel when you bring up the topic of pornography, it may be a good idea to begin the conversation when you are close to home so there can be an imminent escape. But, before even bringing up the topic, consider finding out a little more about what is out there. Today's readily accessible Internet pornography is more intense, explicit, violent, or downright stranger than anything you would probably be imagining.

If younger tweens/teens are frequent Internet users, it is a good idea to set up parental control[11] to reduce the chances of exposure to inappropriate images or videos. Some parental control apps may need a subscription fee with each download but they are good at filtering certain websites deemed unsuitable for the young. Some recommended parental control apps are Norton Family Parental Control, Net Nanny, and Mobicip.

You can also advise your tween/teen to click away from content that is clearly not intended for their age with explanation of the pros and cons of certain stuff that are not meant for leisure viewing. If you think your tween/teen may encounter porn online, either by accident or intentionally, it is a good idea to explain what pornography is in an age-appropriate way. Here are some tips:

1. **Remain emotionally neutral and tell him or her that it is natural to be curious.** This is a hard one, because parents usually have strong feelings upon learning that their child is looking at sexually explicit stuff. If parents react too emotionally or angrily, it increases the tween/teen's shame and he or she is also less likely to listen and to share feelings and all. Remember: It is not an emergency. Take your time to diffuse your own feelings and calm down before you talk to your tween/teen. Avoid saying something that may make them feel ashamed.

2. **Make sure they know you are available to talk about any subject** — and nothing is off limit. It is better to start talking about the birds and bees before they ask their peers or seek online information or misinformation on their own. Talk using positive terms. It is easy to fall into "NO! BAD!" when talking about porn, but it is important to explain the reasons to your tween/teen and encourage him or her to view sex as something good and healthy, and affirm that you actually want them to have good, fun sex when they are adults and/or married. Help them take a long-term view of sex with the goal of a healthy sexual relationship.

3. **Look for other resources** — books, age-appropriate websites, and movies — that can educate your tween/teen about sex, intimacy, puberty, and relationships if the subject proves to be too difficult for any further discussion.

4. **Explain that pornography typically presents the extremes of human relationships** — and that the people depicted are usually paid actors. There can be a frank conversation about the realities (and fallacies) of pornography and the fact that pornography is a production and therefore not representative of the way a typical sexual encounter occurs. It is not representative of real intimacy.

5. **Explain your family's policy on viewing Internet porn** and warn of some porn sites that can invite harmful viruses onto your home computer.

EIGHT

SERIOUS SMARTPHONE AND ONLINE PROBLEMS: DIGITAL HARASSMENT

Digital harassment refers to the use of smartphone, social networks, and other communications devices to bully, threaten, and aggressively badger someone. Although it is a form of cyber-bullying,[12] digital harassment is a bit different because it usually takes place between two people in a romantic relationship.

Parents can support their teens by understanding that relationships these days can be played out both online and offline. Young love is complicated enough without the added pressure of constant access and public scrutiny.

The following tips can aid you in helping your tween/teen navigate these murky waters to prevent any digital drama for themselves and their friends.

1. **Start a discussion.** Your tween/teen may not tell you if harassment is happening directly to him or her. But you can bring it up during dinner chats when you talk about online safety and responsible behavior. You can chat about what you have read from some sources. You can also share with your tweens/teens about some online resources such as Love is Respect[13] and Abusive Relationships.[14]

2. **Let them know you are and will always be there for them.** Remind tweens/teens often that you are always available to talk. Always set aside some time with your tween/teen whenever he or she wants to have a chat or spend a little time with you. Try placing a home communication-notebook or a stick-on notepad for some hand-written notes of encouragement. Do also encourage your tween/teen to call or text you. Even if you are held up at work or in the midst of settling something, always call or text back at the next available time quickly. Try it once to kick-start it and let your tween/teen know that no matter how busy and occupied you are, you can be contacted. Knowing that they have a trusted adult to talk to may encourage tweens/teens to open up.

3. **Help them set boundaries.** Tell tweens/teens never to do anything that is outside their comfort zones, such as sharing passwords or sending sexual photos. (It never hurts to reiterate that anything that he or she sends/posts can travel very far and wide and that "what goes around comes around" sometimes.)

4. **Take action.** If you find out your tween/teen has been threatened or blackmailed, bring the issue to his or her school administrators or law enforcement/police. Although you never want to overreact, your child's safety is the priority.

NINE
HOW TO RESPOND TO HATERS AND TROLLS ONLINE?

Those folks who make cruel remarks just to stir the pot are simply everywhere. Tweens/teens are affected by this to varying degrees, depending on many factors, including his or her age, level of sensitivity, the severity of the comments, and the social situation.

Here are some tips for dealing with the emotional impact and the practical aspects of online haters and trolls:

1. **Explain what it is.** Hating and trolling is a form of cyberbullying, too. This behavior is unacceptable, and there should be no self-blame for what is happening.
2. **Talk about why people act out.** It may be an attention-seeking syndrome for some or it may be because people know they can get away with it, or it may be because the hater is just mean-spirited. Help your tween/teen realize that the comments reflect badly and negatively about these people rather than him or her in reality.
3. **Talk about feedback.** The ability to handle criticism is a valuable skill your tween/teen can use for life.
4. **Focus on the good comments.** Explain that comments are likely to run the gamut from insightful to insulting. Sometimes one can get too fixated on the negative and forget to acknowledge constructive comments.
5. **Help your tween/teen to learn from it.** He or she can learn from the experience that there is a way to respond appropriately and a way to phrase comments constructively.
6. **Explain that your online identity is not your real, true self.** Sometimes, there are people who are hiding behind these identities and one should not take these comments personally.

7. **Be cautious with in-person encounters.** If your child happens to know the troll, the abuse may spill over into real life. If so, make an appointment to speak to that particular person and explain or have a chat over the unacceptable behavior. Or you can speak to other adults — teachers, school counsellors or the parents — to let them know that there is a social situation to be addressed and your own child is a target.

8. **Ignore, block, and unfollow.** Block and unfollow the hater using the site, game, or app's privacy settings.

9. **Flag and report the behavior.** Use the apps' reporting tools to let the companies know someone is abusing their guidelines.

10. **Take screenshots.** If the trolling is threatening, personal, or hateful, save the evidence in case things escalate and report it to the police.

What some teens say:

Tony, *17 years old*

Ignoring really works. Sometimes if you are lucky, you can troll the troll. Sometimes it works, sometimes does not. Don't recommend doing it though.

Kit, *11 years old*

If I am trolled on the Internet, I either ignore it and move on or laugh it off. Sometimes it is done for comedic purposes and should be laughed off when you find out. One thing though — unless it's badly bothering your child, shake it off! Sometimes it is not said correctly or it is for comedic purposes.

> This doesn't even answer the question. On the Internet, we have a saying "Don't feed the trolls", which means that if you don't give them a reaction, they will stop trying.

Tania, *14 years old*

TEN

CYBER-BULLYING: WHAT IF MY TWEEN/TEEN IS CYBER-BULLIED?

Cyber-bullying is the use of digital communication tools (such as the Internet and cell phones) to make another person feel angry, sad, or scared, usually again and again. Examples of cyber-bullying include sending hurtful texts or instant messages, posting embarrassing photos or videos on social media, and spreading mean rumors online.

If you are trying to figure out whether your tween/teen is being cyber-bullied, ask him or her to consider if the offender is being hurtful *intentionally* and *repeatedly*. If the answer is no, the offender might simply need to learn better online behavior. If the answer is yes, take it seriously.

Some tweens/teens may not realize that some teasing are actually bullying in disguise. Some may be too shy or embarrassed to talk to their parents about it. That is why it is important to talk about what the acceptable online behaviors are or appropriate netiquette that your tween/teen should engage in their interactions with others online. To better prepare him or her for such bullies, do these:

1. **Sign off.** Ignore the attacks and walk away from the cyber-bully.

2. **Do not respond or retaliate.** If you are angry or hurt, you might say things you will regret later. Cyber-bullies often want to get a reaction out of you, so do not let them know their plans have worked.

3. **Block the bully.** If you get mean messages through the phone's text messages or social-networking site, unfriend that person or block him or her from the friend list under the privacy setting. Alternatively, delete all messages from bullies without reading them.

4. **Save and print out bullying messages.** If the harassment continues, save the evidence. This could be important proof to show parents, teachers or the police if the bullying does not stop.

5. **Talk to a friend.** When someone makes you feel bad, sometimes it helps to talk the situation over with a reliable, trusted or close friend.

6. **Tell a trusted adult.** A trusted adult is someone you believe will listen and who has the skills, desire, and authority to help you. Let your tween/teen know that telling an adult is not tattling — it is standing up for oneself. He or she can choose to confide in anyone in the family but most importantly, a trusted matured adult.

What some teens and parents say:

Philip, *13 years old*

I know how it feels to want to respond to reach down to their level and say something just as spiteful!!! But you're better so don't bother responding and better still, don't even read into it.

Valerie, *13 years old*

Cyber-bullying is part of life, and we need to know how to deal with it. If someone does start bullying you on social media, you should leave the computer and/or block them. Whatever you do, don't send anything hurtful or mean back. If you do, you are making matters worse. Also, tell an adult you can trust. These are just what I think and my tips.

I would recommend the following: (1) Follow Facebook's age guide line of 13+ age. (2) For Twitter, I recommend a pseudo-account just to be able to get tweets from their favorite star or game and not talk to anyone. (3) If your child "must be in the in-crowd" let him or her create a Facebook or Twitter account and put heavy parental block. There is also privacy setting that he or she can only get friend request and people can't see his or her page or write on it. (4) Tell your child/children that they want a Facebook page they have to add family member(s). (5) Talk to him or her about anti-bully tactics. I think the best is to ignore them. But, if the bullying continues, tell a teacher your child is bullied and the bully/bullies would be sent to talk and explain to the principal or dean of students. (6) Understanding that when your child says "I'm ok" doesn't mean there is nothing wrong. Try to get your child to talk about his or her interest ... and probe further on what he or she would like for dinner. Usually at that point your child would spill the truth out because of the food or the distraction and he or she may actually talk about the "not ok" part. (7) Try to have fun with your kids online. It may sound weird but joining them on the Internet is the best thing a parent could do and to monitor what is said. Learn what's on the Internet that interest them ...

Michael, *late 30s, Parent*

Wilson, *15 years old*

> Just ignore it. Some kids have thick skins and can handle it. I always think they don't like me ... I don't care for them ... why should I let their opinions have any effects on me. More sensitive kids have a harder time handling it, but I think before you directly intervene as a parent, it is important to consult with your kid to make sure they are comfortable with what you are doing. Sometimes if they are being cyber-bullied by someone at school, all it takes is for them to confront them about what they are doing and politely ask them to stop. Most cyber-bullies are just cowards hiding behind a keyboard.

Until recently, parents and teachers have focused on the relationship between a bully and his or her target. But experts say that there are usually more tweens/teens involved in a cyber-bullying scenario, making it a much more complex environment than previously thought. In fact, one of the side effects of how public bullying has evolved is that potentially everyone in the bully's circle of friends — both online and offline — may be involved.

Identifying the different roles in a cyber-bullying situation can help you to aid your tween/teen in developing self-awareness and a sense of empathy. These skills will go a long way toward cultivating an online culture of respect and responsibility.

First, there is the **cyber-bully**, the aggressor who is using digital media tools (such as the Internet and smartphone) to deliberately upset or harass their **target** — the person who is being cyber-bullied. Then there are the **bystanders**, the teens who are aware that something cruel is going on but who stay on the sidelines (either out of indifference or because they are afraid of being socially isolated or becoming a target themselves). But there are also other teens who strongly stand up against such bullying, whether by confronting the bully directly, or notifying the appropriate authorities about what is going on.

Your tween/teen may play different roles at different times. Your advice to him or her will differ depending on the situation and the specific role your tween/teen is playing in the bullying or the drama that is going on.

By making your tween/teen fully aware that a safe world is everyone's responsibility, we are empowered to stand up and stop cyber-bullying. So, do let your tween/teen take positive actions — like reporting a bully, flagging a cruel online comment, or not forwarding a humiliating photo — that ultimately can put a stop to an escalating episode of cruelty.

What some teens and parents say:

> Cyber-bullying is becoming more and more prevalent in today's social media where children are involved. As stated above, there is usually more than two players involved as well. We do tend to think of the bully and the bullied … however, there are more than those two usually involved and when it comes to this, those others involved as the bystanders are just as much a part of the bullying as the person actually doing the bullying themselves. Most children do not realize that they have delved into this modality; and it is prevalent in cyber-bullying as the rest of the bystanders do not want to look weak to the others or be involved in actually being the bully's next target as well. They all gang up on the perceived "weak" one and target them instead, and without thinking of the consequences or evaluating what alternative to doing. All too often, we see our children involved in this and we must take control to stop it. Cyber-bullying is becoming one of the worst epidemics on record and the only way to stop it now is to try to get it at its source. If you have children, it is your responsibility now to monitor what they are doing online, both through computers and through other electronic devices connected to the web. We as parents have to start making sure that we are involved in their lives and know what our children are doing and exactly what they are involved in online. This may seem like intrusion to them, but in the long run we may stop bullying before it starts or we may even save a life from being taken far too soon because of being bullied so badly that the child thinks the only thing to do is to take their life. I implore everyone that reads this and has children to try to be involved in their activities and to make sure they know what they are doing with online discussions and forums that they may be involved in. Remember that it is up to us now to take care of our children both in the real world and online as well.

Mrs Tay, *mid 40s, Parent*

Deanna, *mid 30s, Parent*

First of all, I truly am sorry for all of the children that are being bullied in school. I am a counsellor in a primary school and my number one priority is to prevent bullying. Most victims think that the situation will get worse if they tell someone, but if they get bullied on a daily basis that may be too emotionally painful. If you are getting bullied, TELL YOUR PARENTS AND TEACHERS IMMEDIATELY. Many bullying scenarios can be solved successfully if teachers, administrators, and parents work together. If it's a gang issue, it is more complicated, but there's always a way.

Ruby, *11 years old*

I am a Primary Six girl. I myself was bullied. I have been called several words, terrible ones. Please do tell parents, teachers, or guardians if you are being bullied. Now bullying is getting worse. Take a stand. Speak up. Words can kill. Stop bullying. Maybe someday this world will learn to cooperate.

Educator, *in her 30s*

BLOCK, BLOCK, BLOCK. You have the capability to do that you know!

HOW SHOULD I GO ABOUT DISCUSSING SAFE ONLINE BEHAVIOR?

As soon as your tween/teen begins to go online, it is important to explain your expectations of their behavior. By acting responsibly and respectfully, they will enjoy their time online and get the best of the Internet while mostly avoiding things such as Internet porn, cyber-bullying and inappropriate content. Here are some basics tips:

1. **Communicate appropriately**. Use the right language to communicate with your child. Speak with respect to your child and use the right tone appropriately. Ask him or her to do the same with his or her friends. And never use all capital letters or profanity when communicating with anyone!

2. **Keep private things private**. Ask him or her not to share personal information, including passwords, your home address, inappropriate images, or to gossip mindlessly online.

3. **Respect others**. Gently remind your tween/teen of basic etiquette and to be courteous. If there is a need to disagree, then disagree politely.

4. **Do not lie, steal, or cheat**. Do not try to deceive others. Remember to give credit when credit is due. Do not plagiarize even though it is easy to copy others' works, download things without permission, or use game cheat codes.

5. **Report misbehavior**. Stand up for someone you know who is being bullied online. Knowing the Internet is a giant community, remind your child to help the Internet community to be a nice place.

6. **Follow your family's rules**. Remind him or her of the house/family rules such as avoiding certain websites and being responsible to gain more trust from family members and friends.

7. **Think before posting, texting or sharing.** Discuss with him or her to be considerate of others and to reflect on how he, she or others might feel after having read something in nasty, mean posts. The world operates on a saying of "What goes around comes around" and hence, remind him or her not to "Do unto others what you do not want others to do unto you". Whatever has been said is irreversible and one's online behavior can create a lasting footprint.

What some teens and parents say:

Vivian, *15 years old*

> It's great to take action but, as one with Internet experience would know, trolls are trolls who only want attention ... we should just ignore them. This way, we don't give them the power and they will go away. Anyone knows that the Internet is scary, and there is no way possible to make the "bullying" disappear. I have experienced some things that offended me in the past, but now I find them so lame and meaningless. I think it is best suggest you ask your child what they are interested in and let them find more people who think like them and have the same interest. Otherwise just forget about those meaningless and stupid things written by attention seekers.

> Monitor your kids' account. Ask for permission first. The reason is to ensure that your kid has someone to turn to and let the kid know when they are abusing this. Personally I don't think anyone under the age of 12 needs this stuff. These Internet accounts ... full of bullying and child predators. Sadly, many 11–12 year old girls are posting themselves on Facebook though some innocently and some out to trap the rich sugar daddies. But, where is mom or dad? I think responsibility of parents to monitor their kids' account online is vital and essential in this day and age, especially if your kid is below 12! You will need to ensure the safety of your child! Sorry, but you either monitor everything, or you lose everything. Just in case, being "kiasu" helps. Better safe than sorry.

Mrs Tan, *early 30s,*
Parent to a 12 year old

> We usually think of "It's never going to happen to me". But, seriously, it CAN happen to anyone. Best, is to be aware and be sure your friends know who to turn to for help when necessary. Have your older siblings or friends watch a movie on cyber-bullying. It really hits you hard. Bullying may be taking place to my loved ones or friends as we are talking now.

Melody, *15 years old*

R for
Reciprocal

HOW DO I MONITOR WITHOUT "SPYING"?: A BALANCED APPROACH

When it comes to technology-parenting tip, a balanced approach includes fostering our tween/teen's awareness of media and self, embracing quality media usage, selective single-tasking, carving out times and places to disconnect, and nurturing relationships and face-to-face conversation with our teens. Howard Gardner and Katie Davis[15] point out that media and technology can be especially beneficial when used to form deeper relationships, to allow for creativity and exploration, and to explore identity.

There is a difference between spending time using technology to create digital worlds, hone photography or music skills, or engage in meaningful discussions of important issues and being a passive consumer of content or using technology as a way to distance oneself from social relationships. It is recommended that a healthy digital lifestyle could and should incorporate thoughtful and intentional uses of media and technology.

What is a balanced approach? It calls for prioritizing and focusing on a single task and it is not about multi-tasking with school work or on a social level. A balanced approach calls for essential face-to-face communication on top of online communication with one another to support rich social relationships, be it with our teens, between teens and among our friends, too. Parents can help teens to manage their media uses. As discussed earlier, being a role model of balanced media use ourselves as well as co-engaging media with our teens and having conversations about best media-related practices, strategies and ethical dilemmas with our teens set the relationship and tone right. Parents can also advise on setting limits and drawing up good use of time for what, where, when, why and how to use media. Once these are done, parents can then be their teens' "media mentors".

Additionally, parents would love to ensure that their tweens/teens are safe when engaging in online activities. There are no one-size-fits-all solutions as each and every child is unique and different. But, we can monitor without looking bad. Here are some tips:

1. **Establish a relationship with your tween/teen that you are the one to go to** with any inappropriate or unsettling problem that happens online with the Facebook posts, Twitter or Instagram account.

2. **Have a good heart-to-heart chat as you would with a friend and discuss non-judgmentally about the apps and websites they love.** Ask them to share with you what they enjoy doing and show them you are genuinely interested in what goes beyond their school activities and grades.

3. **Establish a good rapport with your tweens/teens and encourage them to use social media responsibly** especially when they are such sophisticated users of technology. Gently remind them of the dire consequences of irresponsible use as they have such unprecedented access to media and technology.

4. **Be a good digital role model to your tween/teen. Let them see the right netiquette behavior**. If possible, you may request for the password or to add him or her and their friends on Facebook if you wish to monitor their online accounts. But, that said, it is easier to be good friends with them and their friends and have them see the kind of behavior you would want them to look up to and emulate as good netiquette behavior.

Here are some good netiquette behaviors for your tween/teen:

- **Do not flame or name others to shame them**. Think of how you would feel if others were to do the same to you;

- **Consider reading through once again** and also getting a fellow friend or family member to read before posting. This is to ensure no negativity and rebound of feedback and response from others;

- **Be sensitive and do not engage in discrimination** — not being a racist or share crude jokes about other religions or cultural practices and beliefs;

- **Check that tone used is not that of sarcasm** as that would invite more sarcastic remarks and feedback. This would be a vicious cycle that is hard to break;

- **Do not treat social media as an anger-venting machine** to vent pent-up frustration at someone.

What some teens say:

> I don't think that it's right to be checking and sneaking up on your teens. You should trust your teen with the Internet. You should trust them to tell you if they're being bullied or having troubles. Monitoring them makes them feel as if they should do bad stuff. Because if they're not doing bad stuff and you decide to monitor them, then you are pushing him to do all the bad stuff to prove as you're implying that being a teenager, they should rebel. So they will. It's best to leave them alone as they have their rights.

Evan, *16 years old*

> Well if you are added on their FB account, then you can view it but don't embarrass your child by nagging or talking about "mummy talks". And, if you are worried about what your daughter/son is looking at, well, you can always ask directly what they are looking at and what they like to do on YouTube or on Instagram. Not all of us teens like their parents to be online. Not nice to be seen as a mummy's boy or girl. Start by building a good relationship with your child. Let him or her decide if you can be cool to be added. Or just ask directly lah on what they did online or things like that.

Mandy, *13 years old*

THIRTEEN

SHOULD I FRIEND OR UNFRIEND MY TWEENS/TEENS ON SOCIAL MEDIA?

You can ask, but do not insist on it. Some families are connected on social media and it works for them. Some tweens/teens do not want their parents to see everything on their pages (and will block you from seeing things, which kind of defeats the purpose of being friends). Following your tweens/teens online opens up a can of worms, and you will have to figure out how to negotiate that new relationship. If your tweens/teens let you friend or follow them, stay in the background (do not comment or "like" their posts unless they want you to), pick your battles, and make sure to address anything important face to face, not on their pages in front of their friends.

What some teens say:

Mikael, *15 years old*

Yes, "friend" them and comment on their post or pictures if you like. No, if you see something that you don't like or find disconcerting ... DO NOT make a direct comment or response. You can admonish them ... talk to them at home or pull them aside if it truly calls for it. Also be aware that most if not all social media outlets have privacy setting, which means that they can hide many things ... just because you are following them doesn't mean you see everything ... be aware.

Brandon, *16 years old*

If your teen seems comfortable to add you on his or her social media, then that's fine. But for many kids and teens — myself included — social media sites offer a haven away from different forms of stress, such as school and family. If your child doesn't want to be connected to you online: (a) Don't suspect anything of them. Just because they want their privacy doesn't mean they're doing drugs or something. Teenagers often want and even need their space; that's what helps them to function well in adulthood. (b) Understand that they are not trying to keep you out of their life. Life is different for many people ... teens see Instagram as a place to interact with their social friends.

Rebecca, *17 years old*

You just don't like your mum spying on you and knowing everything about you, you know what I mean, right?

Reassuringly, however, according to the interviews with the teens, the majority of teens, that is, 60% of them, said they would tell their parents if something online made them feel very uncomfortable especially the younger ones aged 11 to 14. Additionally, those who received pornographic junk emails, would either tell their friend or parent(s). In essence, some degree of mutual understanding and having good rapport/relationship and open communication are essential to enable such discussions.

FOURTEEN

WHAT APPS ARE GOOD FOR LEARNING?: PROS AND CONS?

With the proliferation of social media and Internet use, we are surrounded by all things techie and there is also no avoiding of these technologies in the learning context too. From guitar to grammar, teens can learn just about anything online through videos, tutorials, how-to's, lectures, and all kinds of different apps. The types of online lessons vary in terms of quality and costs: Some are free; and some have to be paid upfront while some offer a dedicated time, teacher, and subject; and some are simply self-directed (available when you feel like learning something), and of course there are Google and wiki that tell and explain all the questions and definitions.

With the exception of formalized online school, online learning most often happens when tweens/teens search for something they want to learn and check on a video or a wiki to get more information. It is as simple as that to be part of a learning community. The following are some pros and cons of online learning:

Pros:

- It is driven by their passion;
- There is a wide variety of topics to learn from;
- It costs less than a real-world class;
- There is flexibility — at any time and at any place; short or long term;

- Online learning can bring out the best especially for socially shy teens;
- There is flexibility in learning progress — one can rewind, fast-forward, and pause at any pace.

Cons:

- The quality varies;
- The lack of human interaction could contribute to a feeling of isolation;
- Due to the Internet downtimes, it can lead to decreasing interest and quitting midway or a procrastination in learning;
- It needs discipline and it takes a lot to be a self-directed learner;
- There is potential for inappropriate content;
- There is tendency of distractions with all kinds of pop-up advertisements or side bars of comments and URL links.

Nevertheless, here are a few resources for online learning:

- For an unlimited and fun mathematics learning session, here are some websites — http://www.isingaporemath.com/, http://www.kungfu-math.com/, http://www.mceducation.us/math-buddies/ or http://www.thesingaporemaths.com/
- To learn about Literature online, try http://alap.bookcouncil.sg/
- For live online music lessons for all age groups and levels at "Live Music Tutor", access at https://www.livemusictutor.com/
- To learn a language in three months, you can try being "Fluent in 3 Months" — http://www.fluentin3months.com/free-links/
- To learn useful skills on YouTube, try http://tubechum.com/7-useful-skills-you-can-learn-on-youtube/
- To explore various DIY skills — http://courses.diy.org/
- To view a site for teenage girls containing celebrity, music, fashion and entertainment, see http://www.mykindaplace.com/hi.aspx

Online resources for learning are a plenty. There are some good evaluations and guidelines for choosing online resources for parents and tweens/teens and they are summarized here:

1. **Diversity** — Is the content relevant and suitable for different age/social groups?
2. **Accessibility** — Is the content inclusive and does it provide support-group with the media and content accessible to all children of different age groups with different resources and needs?

3. **Interactivity** — Does the content have the interactive potential to enable one to be creative, including creating a community of young people as well as with the appropriate professionals and trusted adults in providing real choices with real consequences?

4. **Educational** — Does the content offer age-appropriate, context-appropriate educational, informational or cultural opportunities?

5. **Value/Quality** — Is it fun and engaging to all tweens and teens and that the content will enable them to want to explore further in terms of formal and informal learning? Informal learning refers to the extension towards life skills and other interests and not just the basic textbook-related content. Does the content provide value in life in the situated context and not just an indirect way of selling the companies' products and services?

6. **Artistry** — Is the content of high quality with excellence in design elements and easy-to-navigate interface?

7. **Safety/Protection** — Are the links safe and carefully chosen with no broken links? Are the requirements for disclosing personal information appropriately managed and does the content advocate or include inappropriate violence or sexual content unsuitable for young tweens and teens?

Are our tweens/teens using these mobile and online resources as a participator or just as a recipient (absorption of information) of these applications/technologies? Why is this valid? Because, by distinguishing among content opportunities, it will serve to better understand the tweens/teens' uses of these applications/technologies and how we can mediate the uses of them for various positive purposes/results.

I have identified two content users: namely Receiver and Participator and the four uses of social media: namely Learning, Participation, Creativity, and Identity. These are shown using the following table.

Receiver
- Learning - Formal & informal e-learning resources
- Participation - Civic & local resources
- Creativity - Diverse arts & leisure & various learning resources
- Identity - Lifestyle & ego-boosting with social contacts/friends

Participator
- Learning - Online practice of activities especially hands-on sessions with no marks/assessment which are also self-initiated and collaborative in nature
- Participation - Invited interaction with active civic engagement
- Creativity - Multiplayer games leading to creative production of skills with user-generated content created
- Identity - Social networking & providing advice to others via peer forum with expression of identity

For the Receiver, there is learning in both formal and informal learning context with both civic and local resources. There are diverse arts and leisure, and other resources for the users. Then through the receiver user mode, teens would feel that it is a lifestyle and ego-boosting contact point to use these social applications to have so many social contacts and friends online.

As a Participator of these social applications via his or her smartphone, there is learning through the online practice activities. There are some activities/sessions that are non-examinable. These activities not only increase creativity with the multiplayer type of games, they are also collaborative in nature. Participation is also active and situated with engagement with the public and the real world. As these applications online are user-generated content hence, there is high level of creativity as well as an outlet for expression of their identities online.

Tweens and teens would also be networking through their peer discussion and forum, which may sometimes provide advice leading to an identity of being a good social counsellor/buddy in terms of identity setting.

IS IT OK TO START HIS/HER OWN YOUTUBE CHANNEL?

It may seem foreign to parents, but for tweens and teens, starting a self-made video is definitely an engaging and fun way to communicate with others. All the coolest apps such as Snapchat or YouTube let users share video clips. So even though you may have concerns about the risks of broadcasting on the Web, it is the norm in today's context. It is what most tech-savvy teens do, especially in expressing himself or herself, learning digital video skills, sharing with friends, and experimenting creatively. It is important to balance your concerns with the benefits he or she can reap from video filming experimentation. There may be a George Lucas — a filmmaker — in the making!

It is definitely a good sign if your tween/teen ask for your permission. So, start by being a good guide and support, and it may be a good fun project for bonding between parents and children. In fact, more and more tweens/teens are using their online channels — whether it is a blog, an Instagram photo collection, Snapchat or YouTube account. These are digital portfolios to showcase their work to employers, universities, and potential collaborators. YouTube even offers free educational content for creators who are serious about their work.

Choose one of the following options for tweens under 13:

1. **Use a parent's account.** If you have Gmail, you have a YouTube log-in. Go to YouTube, log in with your Gmail address, and go to the account settings. Pay special attention to the upload defaults (where you can make your videos private) and the comments, which you can approve before they go live or turn off altogether. If you use your account, you will do all the uploading, but your tweens can still have lots of creative control in the design of the channel, the descriptions, and, of course, the videos.

2. **Create a shared account.** Create a log-in together (or use your Gmail address and add his or her account in the settings). With a shared account, you can review all the steps as a team. Consider keeping the password so you can log in whenever you want.

3. **Use a different website.** YouTube is the most popular video site, but there are also other good options around. Interesting options include: Club Penguin, Time for Kids, Moshi Monsters and Learning Kids Tube, For Kids by Kids.

The following are options for older teens who are interested in creating successful and appropriate YouTube videos:

1. **Have a plan.** Ask him or her to create a proposal for his or her channel that describes what he or she wants to offer, who the audience is, how often the posting is, how about advertising, and other considerations.

2. **Talk about content.** Now is a good time to discuss what is OK to post, what should remain private, and others.

3. **Do a "beta launch".** Take a page from the book of many tech start-ups and start small to work out the kinks. Start with strict privacy settings and a limited audience of trusted friends and family, and ask for constructive feedback on what is working (and not working).

4. **Check in.** Once the video is up and running, continue to support and view the videos. Unexpected issues — both positive and negative — may crop up. Knowing that there is an adult or parent to rely on and to discuss with is definitely a good way for parents to bond with the teens.

5. **Handle feedback.** Teens are often surprised to discover that not everything they upload receives universal praise. YouTube comments are notoriously harsh. But dealing with feedback is a learning experience both for the parents and the teens too.

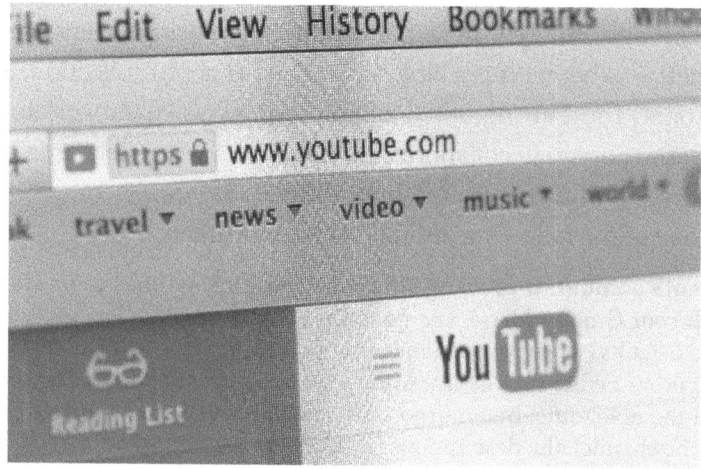

SIXTEEN
MEAN YOUTUBE COMMENTS ARE UPSETTING

Internet trolls — those folks who make cruel remarks just to stir the pot — are everywhere. The best way is to ignore them.

That said, the ability to handle criticism — and learn from it — is a valuable skill that your tween/teen will use for life. Sometimes, knowing what others think of you is the norm, but that does not mean that your tween/teen is ready for negative feedback.

As parents, you can help soften the pain or the discomfort with a pep talk. Explain to your tweens/teens that comments are likely to happen — from insightful to insulting. Remind them to take the feedback with a pinch of salt and use it as an opportunity to evaluate his or her strengths and weaknesses. In fact, your tween/teen can even learn from the experience that there is a way to phrase comments constructively. And if things get too sensitive and uncontrollable with the truly cruel comments, you can report it to YouTube as these negative or derogatory comments violate YouTube's terms of service.

These are some useful tips to use YouTube more effectively:

1. **Use privacy settings.** Set videos to private and choose a small network of people to share with.
2. **Manage comments.** If you post a video, you can either disable comments so no one can write anything, or you can choose to pre-approve comments so you can review them and approve only the ones you want to be visible.
3. **Comment constructively.** Teach your tween/teen to make constructive comments on other people's videos.

SEVENTEEN

CONSTANT MULTI-TASKING DURING HOMEWORK?

Many teens multi-task with social media while doing their homework, and most of them think this has no effect on the quality of their work. In fact, a survey done with some students in Singapore indicated that the majority of teens say they often watch YouTube videos or listen to soothing or rock music while doing homework. In fact, the teens interviewed all strongly feel that listening to music helps them think better and acts as good background inspiration for doing some art homework, for planning a framework and for their essay writing. Some even use social media to post comments, read other posts or just "like" the postings. All of these are done while doing homework.

But, despite what they think and do, frequently multi-tasking affects the ability to focus. Research has shown that many tweens and teens think multi-tasking has no impact on the quality of their homework. As parents, we know that helping tweens/teens stay focused will only strengthen interpersonal skills and school performance.

The challenge for parents is figuring out what is normal (but frustrating) tween/teen behavior and what truly unhealthy study habits are. Listening to music while doing homework seems harmless, but many studies have shown that listening to popular music with lyrics can actually be distracting to comprehension of any subject and even prevent the ability to do complex tasks. But, listening to some calming or Zen-like music or classical music does not. However, if your tween/teen's academic results are slipping, that is definitely a concern.

How to eliminate or reduce multi-tasking? You may adopt the following tips:

1. **Encourage minimizing distractions by managing one task at a time**. Listen to music, say for 20 minutes, and then back to working on homework for the next 20 minutes before the next music break.

2. **Shutting down social media while working offline for homework** or engaging in conversation. Break time calls for social media and not during homework or conversation moments.

3. **Discuss your concerns and talk about ways to structure homework time**, which are strictly no music, game or social media sessions and even switching off the smartphone for a certain amount of time. This is also the best time to charge the smartphone too. Turn on the phone to check texts only after completion of each task or at a set time.

4. **Consider asking your tween/teen to write down assignments** and have him or her check each off as he or she finishes them.

5. **Offer rewards for finishing in a timely manner**, since multi-tasking tends to make homework time drag on.

6. **Look for technical assistance to restrict access at home** at designated time. Do this if your tween/teen is really having a tough time blocking out distractions and staying focused.

7. **Consider a parental control program** or subscribe if your tween/teen is using your home computer to do work that lets you separate homework from playtime.

8. **Read additional tips on multi-tasking and its effects** — https://www.psychologytoday.com/blog/conquering-cyber-overload/201305/is-background-music-boost-or-bummer

EIGHTEEN

HOW TO BE A RESPONSIBLE "INSTAGRAMMER"?

Tweens and teens love using the photo sharing app called Instagram because it lets them apply cool effects and captions to their photos and videos and easily share them across a number of social media platforms. The ability to quickly change the look of their pictures by adding anything from borders to blurring and brightness not only unleashes the tweens/teens' creativity, it also makes their lives look glamorous or just awesome.

One of the biggest draws of Instagram is the instant feedback one can get. Collecting a large number of followers — and flattering comments — is definitely a wonderful experience and an ego-boosting moment to have so many diehard fans following you on Instagram. But, negative comments can be really hurtful. If your tween/teen uses Instagram, make sure he or she knows how to comment respectfully and deal with haters.

Parents also should know that on Instagram, photos and videos are public by default and can contain location data. So it is important for tweens/teens to use privacy settings to limit their audience. Occasionally, negativity crops up, such as so-called "beauty pageants" where users' photos are judged (and losers get a red "X" on their faces).

Also, some teens feel pressured to curate their lives to project an idealized image on Instagram. Sometimes teens create alternate accounts (fake + Instagram) where they share more authentic versions of themselves (in an unattractive outfit or with a silly expression) intended for a close, small circle of trusted friends. Despite these issues, Instagram does a remarkable job of implementing a neat idea with an easy and fast interface, all for free.

Follow these tips to enjoy using Instagram responsibly:

1. **Please set your photos to private**, so that only people you accepted can view your photos.

2. **Stay in control of your online experience, and what you share** (and do not share) with others. You may feel the need to gain more and more followers, and perhaps the best way to do this is to let anyone see all of your photos through your own account and by following hashtags to get to your photos. But amassing more and more followers is a never-ending pursuit, and it can invite mean followers. Hence, filter your followers and hashtags appropriately.

NINETEEN
WHAT SHOULD WE KNOW ABOUT TWITTERING?

Twitter is a microblogging service that features 140-character "tweets" and recently in May 2016, Twitter introduced new functions that allow users to add links, attachments and some other features within the short measure. And as parents, you may not realize how much of a staple it is in tweens/teens' social media lives. According to the Pew Internet survey on Teens, Social Media and Technology Overview, 2015,[16] 33% of all American teens use Twitter and have an average of 95 followers (for teen girls the average climbs to 49% with 116 followers).

What teens like about Twitter is that they can follow (receive tweets from) anyone who interests them, from their best friend to their favorite band and hottest new celebrity — even brands they like. Posts can take the form of text, photos, videos and links. As updates are nearly instantaneous on Twitter, it is like a news service, informing tweens/teens of the information that is most important to them — be it a world event or a school event.

But Twitter has some safety, privacy, and digital footprint issues. Here are some tips to be a good Twitter user and the key concerns to discuss with your tween/teen.

1. **Think through your tweet.** Tweets appear immediately, and — though you can delete them — it is possible that other users could repost or take a screenshot in the span of time it takes to hit delete.

2. **Be as private as possible.** Tween/teen users would benefit from keeping their tweets private and individually approving followers to minimize problems.

3. **Do not use location services.** Twitter's location-sharing features also make it too easy for tweens/teens to post their whereabouts, which has been tied to public-party notices that get out of hand and face-to-face meet-ups with strangers.

4. **Avoid age-inappropriate content.** There are loads of mature content, mature language, and drugs- and alcohol-related content on Twitter, and it is up to users to avoid seeking them out. Twitter is also increasingly being used as a promotional tool for products and services, though users can limit their exposure to advertisements and promotions by keeping their Twitter circles among real friends.

5. **Beware of "sub-tweeting".** Sub-tweeting is when people — usually a group of popular kids at school — use Twitter to gossip about others. Sub-tweets do not specifically say the name of their target, but everyone knows who is being discussed. It can rise to the level of cyber-bullying. Make sure your tween/teen understand why it is hurtful, and teach them to stand up for others.

TWENTY
TUMBLR AND CONCERNS WITH USING TUMBLR

Tumblr is an unending streaming scrapbook of text, photos, videos, and audio clips. It pioneered the vibrant, graphic-rich, full-screen design that tweens/teens love. Interestingly, with more than a million blogs — it is one of the most popular applications on the Web for creative users to design original pages, share cool things they discover, and follow others with similar interests. On Tumblr, the goal of many users is to be "re-blogged" (as opposed to racking up likes, for example, with Instagram), which makes the service feel like a creative community bonded by shared interests. This is definitely not a popularity contest application.

Tumblr is unique because of the wide variety of content that users can post from their phones or computers. Not only can tweens and teens text and post photos, Tumblr also can offer up quotes, links, music, voice messages, and videos. It all shows up on a member's page along with a stream of posts from people they are following. This ability to post instantaneously can be a risk too. What are the key areas to think about before posting?

The key concerns for parents are privacy and inappropriate content. Tumblr posts are public by default. Users also do not have to use their real names (in fact, Tumblr will assign you an interesting username if you do not create one yourself), so you can stay fairly anonymous. On the Web version, you can prevent people from finding you through your email address, but the app version does not offer that setting.

Plus, in all of Tumblr's creative self-expression, it is easy to find both mature content (which you cannot filter) and "advertising" — ads designed to look like regular content.

As with any social networking site, it is important to talk to your tweens/teens about what is OK to post and what should remain private.

The following are tips on using Tumblr:

1. **Do discuss what you can do if someone posts something inappropriate** (for example, reporting that person for violating Tumblr's terms of service).

2. **Help your tween/teen develop media literacy skills by being alert to how advertisers use** a site's signature style to send out their messages.

What some parents and teens say:

Mrs Tan GI, *mid 40s, Parent*

Unfortunately, the big problem with Tumblr is PORN, so if you want to prevent your children from access to it, don't allow them a Tumblr account.

Kit, *17 years old*

My main complaint with Tumblr lies in one of its integral features — the "reblog" button. Re-blogging allows users to post material from blogs that they follow onto their own pages, automatically giving credit to the original poster. Though the intent of this feature may have been to facilitate sharing whatever it is that Tumblr users enjoy viewing — all that it's really accomplished is the systematic destruction of innovation and creativity among the younger generation of Internet users.

> Problem with Tumblr — Porn and near-porn collections for personal use, usually under a different pseudonym. (Protip: Searches on many keywords at 11 pm yield VERY different results than the same searches at 11 am)

Adam, *18 years old*

TWENTY-ONE

SNAPCHAT?: HERE TODAY; GONE TOMORROW?

Tweens and teens love using the messaging app Snapchat because it lets you send texts, pictures, and videos that you program to disappear after a few seconds. Snapchat also offers fun, easy-to-use instant editing tools that let you add cool effects to your "Snaps", such as captions, drawings, and emojis.

The fact that these messages are not lasting makes the whole texting episode feel very game-like and it offer users a weird sense of freedom. Users or tweens/teens can share the silly, fleeting moments of the day that do not rise to the level of, say, an Instagram or even a Facebook post that documents their lives. On the other hand, they may be tempted to share sexy images, thinking the pictures will go away. So not true.

Hence, parents should be aware that it is not actually true that Snaps disappear forever. There is purchase of additional "Replays" although there is a limit to only one Replay per Snap. It is also possible that the receiver could take a screenshot using his or her phone or another app to capture Snaps. This happens in the case of friendship drama or dating/flirting situations. So, parents, please remind your tween/teen to be responsible and to also use good judgment about what they send.

The following is a message from the Snapchat blog team, on snapchat-blog[17]:

"When we first launched Chat, our goal was to emulate the best parts of face-to-face conversation. Chat 1.0 was all about the joys of being here — when most apps told you when your friend was typing, Chat let you know that your friend was listening. Two years later, we've learned a ton about how people talk, but our goal remains unchanged. We want Chat to be the best way to communicate — second only to hanging out face-to-face.

Today, we're excited to introduce Chat 2.0. You can start by sending a few chats, and when your friend shows up, start talking or video chatting instantly with one tap. Your friend can simply listen if you want to sing them a song, or watch if you have a new puppy to show them. If they aren't there, you can quickly send an audio note to say what you mean. And sometimes, a sticker says it best :) ... Happy Snapping!

What we love most about the new Chat is how easily you can transition between all these ways of communicating — just like you do in person. When that's possible, you aren't texting, calling, or video chatting ... you're just talking."

Parents, educators and nearly anyone can have fun with Snapchat given the spontaneity and the fun level of snapping funny shots and emojis, etc. But, no jokes can be funny if certain visuals or jokes are done overboard. There is a need for adherence to basic tact and netiquette to ensure sensitivity to cultural differences, racial harmony, better friendship and relationship, and no ambiguous use of it for unintended purposes to hurt others.

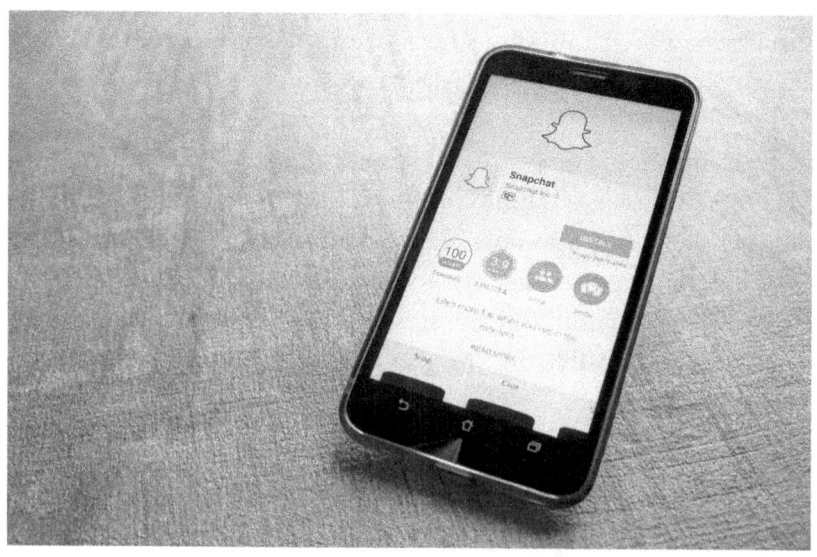

MANAGING EMOTIONS

T for
Tact

TWENTY-TWO

COMMUNICATING FOR A BETTER RELATIONSHIP

How do you have a good and open relationship with your tweens/teens? It would have to start as young as possible to have a healthy and open communication between you and your child. Tweens/teens are going through puberty; teenage angst and these emotions could only be felt vividly by them. I believe, we were young once and most parents have gone through this frustrating tween/teenage phase. Hence, it is time to better understand tweens/teens' sensitive feelings and emotions and try your utmost to understand tweens/teens' growing-up pains as well as their need for privacy as a young adult.

We must learn to accept that our little child/kid is growing up. However much that we would love to have them listen to us as we meant well, we stop giving instructions and orders and try not to use such commands: Do this … Do that … And listen to me … Or you will hear this from your tween/teen: "Stop treating me like a kid!" As a young adult, he or she needs his or her emerging independence, self-identity and as an understanding parent, show respect for his or her choice in life.

Here are some tips to build a good communication rapport with your tweens/teens with these ideas and suggestions as adapted from Anne Cassidy's *Fifteen Ways to Say 'I Love You'*[18] and Ross Campbell's *How to Really Love your Teen.*[19] They are having quality conversation, sharing words of reassurance and affirmation, and spending quality time together.

Quality Conversation

1. **Listen** — **Listen actively and critically** for suggestion. **Listen for content and feelings.** Clarify with "This sounds like you are feeling disappointed … Is it because … Why" or "Are you saying …?"

2. **Ask** — **Ask open and reflective questions** with a "why so?" and a proposal of "how should it be like instead?" **Ask for his or her opinion and choices** like "what would be better instead".

3. **Ask for permission to share your perspective** and have him or her listen to your suggestions, ideas or opinions after having heard his or hers.

4. **Show genuine interest in your tween/teen's activity in school or online** though some topics may seem mundane to you but they mean a lot to him or her.

5. **Do not interrupt or preach** — Interrupting midway or having a sense of your superiority over your tween/teen may seem like a turnoff for some.

6. **Maintain eye contact** — This shows that you are listening. Refrain from rolling your eyes or staring at your smartphone or elsewhere when they are talking.

7. **Focus and show interest in your tween/teen** — Do not multi-task and give your undivided attention when talking with your tween/teen. Quality conversation does not really take a lot of time. A good few minutes of uninterrupted chat would suffice and it can be extended depending on the topic of conversation and the relationship.

8. **Observe body language** — Look out for tense or stressed body language like clenched fists, trembling hands or eye movement, and seek to clarify for such body language and ask for clarification to understand the state of emotion then.

9. **Share a joke or two or confide** in your tween/teen — Try talking to him or her and share jokes like how you would talk with your friends and co-workers/colleagues and you will be amazed at what he or she will share in return.

Words of Affirmation

1. **Begin with "I" and not "You" statement** — "I feel …", "I think …" and "I would prefer …" are words of self-revelation and these are words of informing your tween/teen of your perspective and what is going on. Conversely, "You are wrong …", "You are too young to understand …", "You are making my life difficult …" and "You are making me so angry …" are statements of blame and accusation. Try "I feel angry when …", "I hope you can understand …", "I'm trying to learn new ways of talking with you …" or "I want you to understand my feelings that …".

2. **Use a concerned, conversational and lighthearted tone** to ensure a democratic and not dogmatic conversation. Your tween/teen can have a vote towards the content of discussion too. "Let me share with you what I believe in and then you tell me what you think …" and "I am interested in your opinion …" are appropriate in starting off a conversation.

3. **Offer reasons instead of instructions** — As you listen effectively and attentively, request the same when you offer reasons for your actions and have them hear out your explanation for certain house rules on smartphone uses. They will listen and if they do not agree then, at least they would at least understand your reason(s) for the rules, etc.

4. **Ask your tween/teen** with "What do you think?"

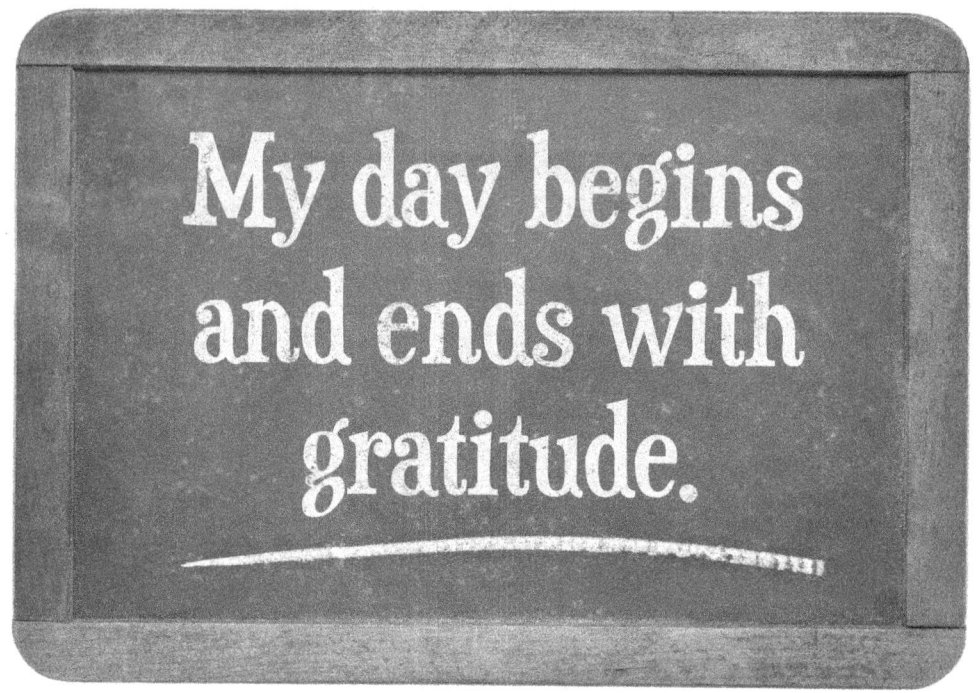

5. **Reassure him or her when things turned out wrong** — No blaming or accusation should be used.
6. **Respect your tween/teen's opinion.**
7. **Tell him** "You are the best son in the world."
8. **Tell her** "You are the best daughter in the world."
9. **Tell him or her how proud you feel of his or her achievement(s); small or big.**
10. **Tell him or her how good he or she looks when he or she takes the effort to dress up.**
11. **Tell him or her that you believe in him or her especially for a new endeavor or skill.**
12. **Leave encouraging notes** — Make the best use of stick-on notes to cheer your tween/teen up if you know he or she is going through difficult times.

Quality Time Together

1. **Plan an event based on your son/daughter's interest** — be it hiking, fishing, attending musical events or visiting places of interest.
2. **Give him or her a video or a scrapbook project during the school holiday for a family event together** if his or her interest is in creating videos or artwork.

Communicating for a Better Relationship 81

3. Take time off to watch a movie of your son/daughter's choice or have a "date-night" with him or her to eat food that both of you would enjoy. Compromise halfway if interests do not meet.

4. Have your tween/teen tell you of places he or she would like to go and why. Then surprise him or her when time is right.

5. Make a simple snack that you think your tween/teen would like and enjoy the eating together.

6. Arrange to pick up or be a chauffeur or be part of the planning team for his or her friends' gathering or party.

7. Keep scheduled times with your tween/teen via your smartphone and make these high priority.

8. If possible, bring your tween/teen to your workplace to better understand your work and to introduce him or her to your friends/colleagues at work.

9. Occasionally, take short walks or bike rides together. Spending time traveling with your son/daughter to his or her school allows for opportunities to spend time together, however short that is.

10. Spend time doing homework together or just doing work separately but at the same time.

11. Eat at least one meal together in a day or almost every day.

12. Attend his or her school events or special day in school.

TWENTY-THREE

Epilogue

My purpose in writing this book is to provide some tips and suggestions to a better understanding of tweens/teens and their uses of the mobile phone. Such understanding is especially pertinent on youth and their connectivity with their smartphone and how best this connectivity can be maximized and leveraged for social networking, as well as serving as a tool for communicating and in building smart relationship between parents and their children. Besides the social reasons of smartphone uses, there is also learning informally and formally with tapping of these technologies.

This book contains anecdotes from parents, tweens and teenagers on the uses of their smartphone and the issues and concerns that they have encountered in the technologically driven society of today. I deeply believe that the most important influence on the tweens/teenagers' choices is parental love and guidance particularly with setting the right house rules with uses of smartphone and other devices and finding ways to spend quality time with quality activities and with appropriate words of affirmation.

The links and websites that one can refer to are included in this book not just for parents but also as a book for educators and others who are similarly interested in reading and understanding what goes on in the everyday lives of youth with their smartphone. I hope that the tips and recommendations can be positively used to reinforce and to build a closer relationship for all. Children are God's gift to us. Treasure them, love them and guide them well especially with the smartphone generation and with the SMART skills recommended in this book.

ENDNOTES

1. Clark, Lynn Schofield (2005). "The Constant Contact Generation: Exploring Teen Friendship Networks Online". In S. Mazzarella (ed.) *Girl Wide Web* (pp. 203–222). New York: Peter Lang.
2. Turkle, Sherry (2015). *Reclaiming Conversation: The Power of Talk in a Digital Age*. New York: Penguin Press.
3. National Addictions Management Services — http://www.nams.sg/Pages/index.aspx
4. Touch Community Services — http://www.touch.org.sg/
5. RescueTime (Android) — https://www.rescuetime.com/
6. Moment (iOS) — https://inthemoment.io/
7. AppDetox (Android) — https://play.google.com/store/apps/details?id=de.dfki.appdetox&hl=en
8. Ask to Buy — https://support.apple.com/en-us/HT201089
9. Excerpts from some of the interviews done with about 50 Singapore teenagers in 2016.
10. Straits Times, 9 June 2016, "Nine in 10 teen boys in Singapore exposed to porn: Survey", http://www.straitstimes.com/singapore/nine-in-10-teen-boys-exposed-to-porn-survey
11. Focus on the Family Singapore Ltd, "Feedback on Recommendations on Public Consultation Paper for Internet Parental Controls", http://www.mda.gov.sg/RegulationsAndLicensing/Consultation/Documents/Consultation%20Papers/Focus%20on%20the%20Family.pdf
12. Wikipedia, The Free Encyclopaedia, "Cyberbullying", https://en.wikipedia.org/wiki/Cyberbullying
13. LoveisRespect Org, "Is this Abuse? Texting and Sexting", http://www.loveisrespect.org/about/
14. Association of Women for Action and Research (AWARE), "Abusive Relationships", http://www.aware.org.sg/abusive-relationships/

15. Gardner, Howard and Katie Davis (2013). *The APP Generation: How Today's Youth Navigate Identity, Intimacy, and Imagination in a Digital World*. New Haven, CT: Yale University Press.
16. Pew Internet Organization, "Teens, Social Media and Technology Overview 2015", http://www.pewinternet.org/2015/04/09/teens-social-media-technology-2015/
17. Snapchat blog — http://snapchat-blog.com/
18. Cassidy, Anne (1997). "Fifteen Ways to Say 'I Love You'", *Women's Day*.
19. Campbell, Ross (2004). *How to Really Love Your Teen*. Colorado Springs, CO: David C. Cook.

www.ingramcontent.com/pod-product-compliance
Lightning Source LLC
Chambersburg PA
CBHW070347100426
42812CB00005B/1450